GIFTS FROM THE INDIGENOUS

Another Way of Viewing & Acting in the World

Michael A. Susko

AllrOneofUs Publishing
Baltimore, Md & Huntsville, Al

While every precaution has been taken in the preparation of this book, the publisher assumes no responsibility for errors or omissions, or for damages resulting from the use of the information contained herein.

GIFTS FROM THE INDIGENOUS: ANOTHER WAY OF VIEWING & ACTING IN THE WORLD

First edition. November 7, 2024.

Copyright © 2024 Michael A. Susko.

ISBN: 979-8227049001

Written by Michael A. Susko.

For our world which is infused with Presence

Introduction

My interest in the Indigenous world came about because of my own symbolic experiences. In my early attempts to understand these experiences as a college student, there seemed little that was relevant or affirming in my study. Perhaps the closest were from psychologists like Carl Jung, who explored an array of archetypes. However, I eventually found that Indigenous worldviews resonated best with my experiences, providing examples of direct contact with the symbolic/spiritual world. I am reminded too that my own "vision quest" started after walking all night in the rain and ending up in Moundville, Alabama, a sacred Indigenous center.

More broadly, I believe the Indigenous world view can serve as an important compliment to our Western mentality. Currently, we are discovering the limits of the traditional Western world-view. It has an unconscious pull toward believing its mentality is superior, which leads us to more easily abuse the earth, oppress "lesser" peoples, and veer us all toward authoritarianism. In short, we find ourselves on the path of destroying the earth. Alternative visions are needed to pull us away from this dark path. Perhaps unexpectedly, we are called to pay attention to the ongoing historical power of the Indigenous, their vision, and to the sacred geography still embodied in this land.

My awareness of the Native American Indigenous vision has been largely gained by several years of academic study and teaching classes about the meaning of its symbolism. It has been furthered by finding a "Mystery Stone" by the Shenandoah River in Virginia, and a publication last year which documents months of intense interaction with this stone. This was recently complimented by a visit to Penn Bluff in Alabama, where I unexpectedly came across a monolithic stone formation, which to my mind's eye has an anthropomorphic-bird-like shape. I will draw upon these two examples to illustrate six awarenesses and six actions the Indigenous worldview can gift to us.

This work does not provide academic citations. Rather, it offers an informed meditation that arises from my experiences and study. My hope is that this work can aid in our journey toward greater consciousness and to further discovery, which will help bring a healing presence to the world.

Over twenty years ago, I found a "mystery stone" among a clearance cairn in the Lower Shenandoah Valley. Immediately, I saw markings which made for a curious design, and strongly felt the thought, *"This is my gift to you."* After teaching Indigenous studies for many years, this stone finally inspired me to write and to share the vision it presented to me.

But perhaps one stone is not enough. This past summer, visiting a close, artist friend, I was encouraged to visit a landscape in the rural hinterland of my home state of Alabama. As I came across a bluff with a monolith stone formation, I felt a strong sense of presence and resonance with Indigenous symbolism. This I take to be a second gift, which has inspired me to write this work, and which I now offer to you.

SIX AWARNESSES

Spiritual Pervasiveness

One basic belief of the Indigenous World is that the spiritual dimension pervades this world. Perhaps this best example of this is the beauty of the landscape with all its plants and animals. The ancient Aztec word for this universal presence was *Tonalli*. Despite all the diversity and variety of the world, there is an essential oneness envisioned. This oneness is more fundamental than anything dividing or separating things. Thus, we can, in this view, envision matter as having a type of life. The anthropologists and those who proselytize an orthodox religion have viewed this belief with a negative connation, as an early stage of spiritual awareness called *animacy*. Rather than comparing ideas or views as one as being truer than the other, we can see what beauty or truth a given belief may have.

In this openness to seeing or feeling a pervasive spirituality in all things, how would we change? It seems for one, we would be more accepting, more open to things. It seems like the slightest current of spiritual winds would be able to pass through us. We are out in nature and we are open to the energy of the land. Persons have sensed what they call hotspots, where they move, view and feel in their interaction with stone, trees, and water. These three elements have been viewed as present in sacred spots.

Recently, I viewed a site at Penn Bluff and Creek in Alabama. My elderly monk friend of decades still works on his art and architectural designs, though he is in the infirmary. One of the caretakers has a fascination with stones and sees a variety of Indigenous imagery present in them. They have found a variety of arrowheads on the property, but there were no Indigenous designs that I could discern on the stones, though they were interesting. The stones to her, however, had a type of animacy and life that resonated with her being, and I respected that. They did not have to have Indigenous markings to make them sacred. In the Indigenous view, the natural world is already considered to be sacred.

She did, however, have interesting rock formations on her land that presented a monolithic beauty. While walking, we came upon a formation that they hadn't noticed and which presented a remarkable natural sculpture. At first it looked unknown but fascinating, then it came into view as a frozen stone waterfall. As it was examined more frontally, a strong anthropomorphic feel came into view, and then the birdman archetype.

As I was photographing, the doors of wonder kept opening. I was seeing a lot but did not know all that I was seeing. Such is the scared that it has a type of infinite depth, that it presents only a facet or two at first, but then keeps opening doors and revealing.

So sacred energy can be viewed as everywhere, but it comes with intensity at certain moments and places. We might envision that the general attitude of being open to the sacred and feeling it on lesser levels everywhere enables us to be ready for a fuller influx and experience.

So, we have the paradox of sacred energy being everywhere, yet certain places and times we feel are more infused with than others.

Chapter II

Mothering Earth

All things we see in this world must be born and mothered to exist. Our dependence is from moment to moment, as we breathe, as we absorb warmth from our surroundings, as we burn energy from food taken from outside of ourselves. We might be aware of or readily remember this basic reality, yet it is obvious, and a fact of existence. The Indigenous turn our attention to this mothering principle, with their many images and stories of the female archetype, which features her gift of abundant blessing.

There are famous images which embody this principle. A rotund female holds a lunar shaped horn from the Paleolithic site of Laussel, France. From Cahokia in Illinois, the central cultural site of North America, a figurine has been found: a kneeling woman wears a pack of sprouting gourds and holds an adze which plows a sacred snake. Complexity and narrative are present in the story of the Great Mother, but we must not miss the principle. The mother births and nurtures life. If we do not care for the mother, we will destroy the earth and the lives she shelters. That life, especially in its incipient stages, is fragile. Without the mother, we would not have life, nor the evolution of life.

We may think of the mothering as painting the world with a rosy color and not integrating the shadow side of reality. But the mother sacrifices, risking her life to birth new life into the world. In the Green Corn ceremony of the Native American Southeast, there is a celebration of harvest and renewal of the earth's annual cycle. An associated Cherokee story has the corn goddess drug seven times around the field, her death linked to the land's fertility.

In Western Civilization there is a constant danger of undervaluing or dismissing the mothering principle. Consider this example. One name for the Hebraic God was *El Shaddai*, which translators have variously interpreted, including "God of the Mountain." Its use in scripture was with blessings of fertility, celebrating and giving thanks for the fruits of the land. At least one scholar believes it is related to the word *Shadayim*, the Hebrew word for breast, consistent with its use in fertility blessings. When the word came over into the Greek, it became *Pantocreator*, or the creator of all things. In Latin, an empire culture, it became *God Omnipotent,* or all powerful. In English modern times, with the continuation of empire, it became *God Almighty.* Thus, the mothering aspect of Deity was turned into an opposite meaning. It's not that the opposite does not hold its truth, for mothering brings a type of power, but we do not want to miss or obscure its essential meaning.

We are all mothered when we are young, and our helplessness and need for mothering is an essential aspect to our evolution and greater consciousness. And it continues throughout life. We never at any point become self-sufficient, where we do not need the blessings of a good environment or others. We are not God. This latter point is a great temptation, to think we should aspire to rule the earth and others. Rather, we are here to mother others, not to rule them. Of course, rules are enforced, especially for safety. But it is not the essence of the mother archetype. And when rules are necessarily enforced, they are done as a loving act for the other.

As we emerge from empire's unconscious frame of mind, where kings, rulers, and presidents are glorified, we are prompted to develop the feminine mothering dimension of our being. This includes males. When I had my only child, I took off leave for the second three-month period between 3-6 months, as leave did not have to be taken immediately after birth. In that time I intimately cared for my son and a bond was created that has lasted into the teen years. At the time, I thought that if men did this, they could not go to war. For they would realize the preciousness of the child, and not one child should be killed. One child is worth more than all the gold in the world, for there was no price that I would sell my son.

In the past few decades, archeologists have been unearthing the history of humans, before the massive empire constructions, often built by slaves. Over periods of thousands of years, more humble homes and villages have been found, often clustered in circular mounds. A plenitude of mothering figurines has been found in such households, which continued as an underground religion even when the Kings declared themselves gods.

Our early humanity and the Indigenous remind us to keep close the mothering archetype or principle. It is something we may not aspire toward, reflect much about, or give thanks for, but it is so pervasive that our existence depends upon it.

Mediation often starts with becoming aware of breath. We breathe oxygen released by plants which exist in the mothering earth. There are air plants which are not rooted in soil, but their leaves absorb moisture and minerals from the air. We cannot escape the mothering principle, nor should we try. The wisdom of the Indigenous points us to that enduring truth.

Chapter III

Tripartite Division

The traditional Indigenous division of the cosmos is into three worlds: the Netherworld, This World, and Overworld. This is a useful way to construct the world, to make sure we integrate energies on these three levels. While teaching at a progressive elementary School, for which I was a founder parent, we explored this once in an arts integration lesson, in which you equally teach the principles of two disciplines. We were teaching the three main types of clouds: stratus, cumulus, and cirrus, and at the same time the three levels of dance. You can dance with the energies of the lower body, middle body, or upper body. As we did this, we had the children dance at each level, matching the corresponding level of clouds.

In a like manner, we envision benefit to incorporating a tripartite understanding, to achieve a holistic vision and balance to the world. Let us review these three levels and see what energies are associated with them and how they are valuable to us.

Netherworld

The Netherworld looks at things below the surface. In the landscape, it presents as caves, sources of springs, and places underwater. The energy here is double edged, for it is both life giving and dangerous, with the capacity to kill and to birth things new. The two can be integrated, for dissolution can be seen as the first stage in a transformation which births new life.

The forms of the Netherworld often appear to be confused and inchoate, not easily defined in the normal scheme of things. The word *inchoate*, however, means incipient states of something new. Out of the chaos and uncertainty of the forms of this dimension, we can witness the rising of clearer definition and form.

It turns out that the Netherworld has its own hidden structures and rules which are not commonly accessible to our everyday mentality. It is like the meaning of dreams, which follows patterns and structures, yet are typically opaque to us.

In the Netherworld, the beings that present are often composite, such as the Eastern Woodland *Ukteni*, which is typically snakelike with a horned animal head. Unusual hybrid beings, outside of the normal order of things, can arouse fear in us. Meeting unusual, unexpected forms is part of the mystery of This World, and is encountered on the edges of human experience. Incorporating this shadow side of reality can be among the most difficult and neglected tasks of our lives.

We are in danger of being manipulated by those who would paint this shadow side on other groups of people, in which broad groups of persons are scapegoated due to artificial reasons such as race, country of origin, or political beliefs. The challenge is to integrate this Netherworld dimension and see that it is present in our own selves, and to avoid projecting it upon others so that we gain permission to harm them. We are invited to be procreative and generate life, to direct our energies to love and making love, rather than to hating, war, and destroying life.

The Netherworld is the lower part of the design, the foundation on which things rest. Our legs and pelvis drive our movement and provide our stability and balance in the world. It is also the area of generative force which makes for new biological life. At the base of the rock formation at Penn Bluff, cupules underlie a dome upon which our anthropomorphic-like figure stands. They are like the eggs at the base of forming new life, or the incipient thoughts that are ready to rise to consciousness. The Indigenous invite us to integrate and become aware of the Lower World dimension. We are invited not to neglect that which is a rich source of creativity and new life.

Yet, dangers are present here. One becomes vulnerable if one fully immerses in This World. Predatory persons/forces will try to take advantage and victimize people going through such experiences. Commonly, they are mistreated badly, given powerful medical treatments that serve to diminish one's life force and stop the transformation process.

Fully experiencing the Netherworld may be conceived as a once in a lifetime event, or a rare occurrence. It can also be seen as a continuous stream operating within us, which surfaces to consciousness at times, as during the night with dreams or during crisis.

In the Jungian view, unexpected gold and richness are found in properly harnessing this dimension. It is like the dwarves in mythology, in which smaller, seemingly more misshapen beings, mine the riches of the deep earth. We are invited to consider that our inspiration comes not only from on high but from the Netherworld dimension. Historically, we have been tempted to reject these energies, as with various forms of Gnosticism and Jansenism, which believed the body to be evil. But the body is good and we must learn from all the energies present. This does not mean that we cannot abuse or misdirect our bodies. But we can integrate the varied energies of the body, from lower, middle, and high, to make for a holistic life.

Let us move to the next dimension of *This World, or* the *Middle World,* and the place of the heart.

This World, Middle World

This World, or the Middle World, is where we typically find ourselves. It is the world of landscape with plants, animals, and people which offers beauty and places practical demands upon us. This World we come to know well enough, but in relation to Indigenous cosmology, it also has portals through which other worlds are entered. These involve transformations of our being, which we will deal with under a separate heading. For now, we will focus more on the horizontal dimension of This World.

Typically, This World is seen as embracing four directions each which has a distinctive feel and symbology. Let us explore these directions, keeping in mind an Indigenous awareness and our own sense of direction in a temperate zone. The excursus below is an invitation for us to consider our own sense of directions and what they might mean to us. We are, in essence, making a mandala that helps to orient us in the world. The gift of the Indigenous is to invite us to consider this. Here, I will draw upon the two examples of the portable mystery stone and a monolithic stone formation that served as portals for me to experience and understand the Indigenous view.

1. <u>The East:</u> The east is the place of dawning, of the rising sun. Things birth and come to life then. The night is slain, and the morning star rises as a precursor to victory over the dark. In Eastern Woodland cosmology, this was viewed as a time of combat by a military leader. It is reminiscent of the victory at dawn of the Exodus, when the Egyptian army is swept away by the Red Sea. In the Mystery Stone from the Lower Shenandoah, the beaked head of the anthropomorphic figure faces east, toward a leaping feline figure. Thus, birthing is mixed with

danger and precarious entry into the world. A color that is fitting for the East, with its association with the sun and birthing, is yellow.

2. <u>The North:</u> The North has associations with dark, cold and harsh winds. It can be viewed as the place that precedes birthing, an inchoate place where forms are born. Thus, underworld associations overlap here. In this wilderness we are distant from a more structured, constrained society, and so it has associations with freedom. Yet danger is present here as we enter more liminal zones, where hybrid creatures can arise. Here one experiences trials, faces tests and is ultimately cleansed. A color that might fit this symbology is black.

3. <u>The West:</u> This direction precedes from the East, where the sun starts and then ends in the West, bringing darkness across the land. Though this area could be envisioned as black, I choose the color red, fitting archaic Woodland cosmology. Red is the color of death and rebirth. Death is envisioned as not permanent, but as a period of passage. The enduring state is one of new being, and the West envisions a passage to this state. With the anthropomorphic-like form at Penn Bluff, its west side has a stream of red flowing out or into the base of the form. On the Mystery Stone, there is the dark red form of a serpent hybrid being that crosses the stone and enters rising in the West, presenting a bearish head, symbol of rebirth.

4. <u>The South:</u> The South is perhaps the most novel reinterpretation of our sense of direction, using a temperate Eastern Woodland cosmology. The reality is that the sun shines from this direction throughout the entire year, but especially in the Winter where it hangs perilously low on the horizon. Houses, habitations, shrines all do well face this direction to be present for its light and warmth. Our anthropomorph at Penn Bluff is facing South, the whiteness and light colors standing

out in the winter light. In the mystery stone from the Shenandoah, the top area is lighter. The color of this zone may be viewed as white.

Intersection of Directions & the Cruciform Design

In terms of anthropomorphic form, the Middle World can be seen as one of a cruciform torso. It can be envisioned as a torso, standing with arms extending into the world, manipulating and embracing things. One of the most common symbols, if not the most common, in the Southeast ceremonial complex is the cross and circle design, symbolizing the four directions. Our anthropomorphic form at Penn Bluff presents such a sense. We can see extensions on both sides, suggested by the crossing of the undulating form.

The center of this cruciform world, the torso of the anthropomorph, is the heart. It may also be envisioned as midday sun, giving forth its expansive light and warmth across the world.

In sum, we are invited to embrace the world in all its dimensions, from birthing to death/rebirth, from the place of dark and trials, to the place of light and warmth. It is a cosmology written into the world.

Overworld

The Overworld orients us to the heavens, the stars and sun. It is the direction to which things are growing and aspiring toward. It is the region of the head, with its senses, and projections from the head. In the Mystery Stone, there are lines leading up from heads and patterns to the top of the Stone, ending in designs which may be stars, flowers, or hands. In Southwest and Mayan cosmology, it is the region of the *flower world,* a place of iridescent beauty. Flowers as the upper parts of plants can be seen as belonging to the upper domain, just as leaves and stems can be viewed as This World, and roots as connected to the Netherworld.

In the apparent anthropomorphic form at Penn Bluff, Alabama, there is a head with horned projections that flow into arches above. The head has a beaklike form on its top, and its torso like horizontal extensions call to mind wings. It echoes the pecked form in the Mystery Stone, which shows beaklike forms as well. The bird and shaman bird-man are central Indigenous archetypes of the Eastern Woodlands, beings which can ascend to the celestial realm. Often, they go there to find wisdom and energy, to bring back healing and beauty to the community. Energies that lift us upward, to a beyond, to the future, to what is not yet, and to what is becoming are the stuff of the Overworld.

The South, as a direction, has Overworld associations. As already noted, the South is the dominant direction of the sun, bringing us light and warmth. My more direct experiences of God's love have come at night in a dream-like state or in dark places like a deep cave, as a strong feeling of warmth and light through my body.

The Overworld has associations with the arch and mountains. The top of the mystery stone forms a rough arch, and its projections look like mountains in miniature. The anthropomorphic like form at Penn Bluff has arched projections over it, and can be seen as a "mountain" in miniature. The arch and mountain lift our eyes from the earth to the upward domain.

On top of the mystery stone from the Shenandoah, there appears to be a hand and eye form, a common SE ceremonial symbol. It might represent a portal or a symbol of a being in the upper dimension. The eye sees and the hand touches elements which may be present in the being above. The disarticulation points to a mystery to this being, as something more than we can imagine.

The Overworld realm invites us to imagine, to go beyond our current conceptions. We can imagine a world of intense, almost unbearable beauty, awash in light and warmth. It is the domain of pure love, a point and place to which our world aspires and to which we all hurl.

Chapter IV

Tension of Opposites

The Indigenous Vision gives prominence to the place and importance of opposites. In nature and the world, things can be viewed as being paired. For example: day-night, male-female, sky-earth, warm-cold, and so on. This does not mean that there are not twilight zones and variation within a binary pattern and that society must come to grips with in-between states. Thus, we may see opposites as being in tension and producing offshoots. In a vision that embraces opposites, these pairings can see as intertwined and their tension creating something new.

Pairings and contrasts also serve to make things clear. Foils are often present in the structure of dreams, for example. The first scene may show you alone, struggling to pass through a series of obstacles. The second scene may then show you with a group encountering a different set of tensions. The contrast between the two serves to hold the two together and give one unexpected insight into their unity. In this case a fuller picture of ourselves embraces our solitary and social dimension.

Archetypal figures also present as foils. In a shamanic journey, the Birdman ascends into the Overworld. He is contrasted with the snake-like hybrid who dwells in the Netherworld with its set of treasures. These two beings may be in combat, or in a creative tension which can produce a life-giving result. In the case of the earth mother, the woman figurine hoeing the snake, the action produces fertility.

The saying "Love your enemies" in a type of embrace of opposites. Perhaps this is the most difficult of spiritual teachings, for it is counterintuitive. Your enemies seek to diminish you and take life away from you. How does loving them alter that dynamic? If love, or the bond between opposites and opposition, is greater than the hate or enmity between them, then we can say that love will ultimately win. The mission is to convert the cold reaches of the universe into the embrace of love and warmth. This can be done by first recognizing the opposite, seeing our bond to the opposite, and then reaching out and engaging the opposite. If an opposite is transformed by this contact, a tremendous energy can be released and much good can be done. After Saul of Tarsus, who killed his supposed enemies, was thrown off the horse of empire, he bonded with his "enemies" and so converted the Gentile world.

The embrace and transformation of opposites are one of the great mysteries of our world. It is one that many refuse to see, leaving us to fall more easily into the cycle of exclusion, hate, and violence. We are called to enter the mystery of opposites and to unleash its power for the good of the world.

Chapter V

Transforming World/Body

An important, neglected wisdom from the Indigenous is the transforming/ changing nature of the world. The ideal is not a static, immovable perfection like a Greek God or Goddess, set in ideal proportions, which once obtained, do not further change. Rather, our being moves and dances. The anthropomorph, detailed in the Shenandoahan stone, conveys movement, thrusting its body forward, his balance shifting. He can be seen as in the process of becoming, transforming. The face has an indefiniteness in the mouth area, in which there are many possible beaks or projections, suggesting its face is transforming. Likewise, the anthropomorphic form at Penn Bluff has a face from a lower angle, but from the side, its beaked projection brings a bird like aspect to the torso. This alteration between archetypal birdman form and anthropomorph invites us to be keyed to transformation.

We know from the cycles of nature that things are constantly transforming. The sun gives light and energy, which plants use to convert carbon found in air into plant substance of leaves, stems and roots. If this is true on the physical level, why is not such transformation present on the psychological and spiritual level? Such is the Indigenous vision, which sees these various worlds as emerging from fields of relationships and in a constant state of renewal and transformation.

The moment of transformation is easy to neglect. It happens momentarily and we are more satisfied to see set, end results. We are geared to take aways, not how we get to that point. When the change is actually happening, we may only be partially aware, or conscious. How does this process of change occur? What happens when our being transforms?

I found this true in evolutionary study. Scientists are geared to the end result of evolution, to the fit creature that has survived and established itself. The moment of evolution, the vulnerable time itself, the period of fragile change, we avert our gaze. Why is this?

Perhaps the reasons include that change and transformation are near invisible. The processes involve forces, of which we are only partially aware. Perhaps too, it is confusing, involves a painfulness in the growing consciousness of new being. If we become something new, persons don't recognize us, think we're strange and unconsciously pull away, or try to draw us back to our old ways of being.

Those who would control others with an empire frame of mind fear and avoid the transformative vison. A transformed human does not make a good slave, or someone easy to manipulate. The major world religions, to their credit, have keyed on the change process as an essential dimension of reality and their vision. In Christianity we speak of conversion, a turning around. Buddhism speaks of enlightenment. In archaic Eastern Woodland vision, the concept of "bone-soul" is tied to transformation. Rather than the soul essence being a set shape, we are invited to see the soul as something pulsing, moving, and dynamic.

If we envision our essence as embracing change, as rising like a fountain which leads to new being, we are "loosening up" our sense of self, allowing for the new to emerge. Perhaps it can even be toward our better self.

People can certainly transform for the worse. It is one of the great disappointments of life to see persons and aspects of the world take a turn for the worse. It does, however, point to a radical freedom and a movable nature that can change.

Despite this emphasis on flux and change, we do not mean to conclude that we are chameleon in nature and don't have a type of centering soul essence. Perhaps this transformation awareness it is best viewed as part of a tension of opposites. The touchstone or essence of our being stands in contrast to dynamic movement that would cause our essence to evolve further, to transform into the new.

Chapter VI

Shamanic Bone-Soul

In this section I return to the meaning of the bone-soul and the shamanic dimension of this reality. That our essence, something vitally important, is connected to bone is a primordial awareness of humanity. For all the spiritual heights and the soaring consciousness of humankind, there is a rootedness in bone. Spirituality is embodied. There may be beings who are not embodied, but all consciousness that we readily discern is accompanied by a body. When one attempts to meditate and access other dimensions, realities or perceptions, one becomes very aware of their body.

Bones serve as the scaffold, the foundation, and mineral support, which allows us to stand and move in the world. While in an altered state for weeks, I recall my own experience of feeling/seeing an intense whiteness vibrating from the bones in my arm. It was as if the spirit residing in the bone became manifest, revealing the presence of the soul-bone. Everyone has this gift of bone-soul, a substance making for dynamic life within us. This bone-force is connected to the spirit world, to forces beyond itself.

The shaman accesses this bone awareness and uses it as a ladder or portal to reach spiritual heights. Often, portrayals of shamans are rendered in partial skeletal form, as they fly upon this magic carpet of bone. The shaman accesses the bone's transformational power, a half-dead, half-living state which makes his or her passage possible.

Normally, we are not so much aware of our bones unless they are hurting. Their fluidity and continuity with our enfleshed being are a marvel of being/evolutionary gift. It is a great mystery how meditation and connection with them can open doors to spiritual realities and our evolutionary future.

Bones have a geometric dimension which makes use of golden proportions. They are fluid and functional, with marvelous mechanics able to give flight to some creatures. In a sense they are the obvious geometry and abstraction of our body. This skeletal dimension, separated from flesh, suggests death to some, but it can also be viewed as a diagram of our soul-being. For within this network of bones, which is enfleshed, there is another physical reality we have yet to mention. That is, flowing electrical forces pulsate and originate from the bones and organs within us. This energy may be seen and felt, often in the dark, by our "third eye." In laboratories, scientists can photograph this energy in creatures, revealing its rainbow spectrum.

That matter can come alive and be harnessed by life is unexplained. That living matter can become conscious of itself is likewise unexplained. Finally, that alive and conscious matter is connected to spiritual forces beyond itself also remains a mystery. These three great mysteries are experienced when one touches and comes into contact with the bone-soul.

It does not end here. For each of us has bone-souls and they can, through love, be joined into an overarching soul-body. This would lead us to yet a seventh awareness, as the list awarenesses do not end. Rather than explore this directly, we will move to the doings which come from the awarenesses and which are acts of love.

SIX DOINGS

29

Vision Questing

The first doing is to quest. At certain ages and times, we find ourselves more intensely seeking. It means we feel there is something more that we must explore and take risks, and go beyond our normal ways. In the 60s counterculture, it involved taking mind-altering substances and separating from normal accepted ways. In Indigenous America, it involved going to a remote location, fasting, and "crying for a vision." If we go through life and do not find our unique vision of what we are called to do, then we risk living a life that is not our own and a tool for secular powers that would use us for their profit. We are meant to go back and give to society, but it is essential first to go off and find the vision. In the archetypal hero story, as with Jesus, we find him going off into the wilderness to battle demons and consort with wild animals and angels, all before his mission in the world.

This basic doing should not be omitted in our lives and the lives of our youth. Oftentimes when people struggle in this encounter, it is misunderstood as a deviance to be stopped and shut down, rather than protected and guided. It is a great failing of our contemporary society to pathologize the vision quest. Not only does it choke off visions that would enable our society to survive, but it harms innumerable youth. The great oath that medicine and parents should take is to do no harm. Yet that is precisely what is done, whether wittingly or unwittingly. Giving numbing drugs, electrical shock treatments, and *stop-experiencing* therapy as a routine matter and lifetime solution to the emotionally vulnerable and vision questors is a great unspoken tragedy of our times.

In the Indigenous view, such transformational states are protected, and if substances are used, they serve to encourage the altered state, not stop it. Like in all history, there is more than one current going on simultaneously. In this case the undercurrent looks for meaning in symptom expression and helps the person come to their more actualized self. For example, smaller scale alternative homes have arisen, which allow persons to go through their transformative process. In harmony with this, recent mental health treatments have incorporated psychedelic therapies to facilitate the transformative process that our youth naturally undergo.

Despite the dominance of mainstream resistance, the vision and the questor breaks through. What is sought, the reality that the vision aspires to, is much greater than the forces arrayed against it. The vision cannot be stopped, but a lot of damage can be done to persons in the interim along the way. And for many, we can only hope that after death or a foreshortened life, the vision is finally realized.

When I was 18, I left the University of Alabama campus and walked off into the dark on one rainy night. Leaving behind my experimentation as a freshman, I walked until exhaustion, ending up in Moundville, Alabama some thirty miles away. When I woke up, I was in a visionary state, experiencing Aztec light, the sound and sight of trains surrounding me with the strong thought, *"The morning trains have risen, but no one is guiding them."* From there, I entered a symbolic world for several weeks. Fortunately, the psychiatric who treated me allowed me to go through my symbolic experience. Afterwards, I experienced a classic conversion experience involving fasting and healing experiences with Christianity. Thus, my life's touchstone is interwoven with visionary, Indigenous awarenesses, and my historical religion. Having and incorporating a symbolic visionary experience led me to live a fuller life, in which the whole community gained. If there is one basic doing we should allow, let our youth find their vision.

Chapter II

Mandalic Walking

The second doing is to possess a map of our world and to walk it. What is on our map? What are the main elements and types of things you experience when you journey? We have already discussed a tripartite division of the world, in which This World possesses four directions with symbolic and experiential value. Typically, a mandala has at least four major elements with a center. For example, our temporal life can be viewed as having four stages: youth, adulthood, middle age, and senior. There is also a center from which we emerge, infancy/beginning, and go toward death/renewal. In our life we walk these stages.

Thus, the first step is to become aware of the mandalic nature of things, a sense of how our universe is meaningfully constructed. Once we possess this map, we take steps to make sure we walk it. We must walk the talk. There may be a section of the mandala we fear and have avoided walking. This should be visited. We may be spending too much time in one area which ends up distorting things, for we have neglected its opposite. The *enneagram,* a mandalic mapping of personalities, features this type of awareness. For example, a person may be strong in having vision, but is weak in leadership that would share the vision. The goal is to actualize our full being, which takes an attendance to the full mandalic reality.

When I was in college at a small Benedictine school in Alabama, I edited a literary journal, which included a work of a mandalic construction. The stages I mapped were 1) the mother/earth dimension for childhood; the 2) father/thought dimension for emerging adulthood; 3) A transformational stage of positive withdrawal, compared to the chrysalis stage of the butterfly, where one became aware of symbolic/spiritual reality and 4) a flowering, spiritual blossoming in the world, like the Imago or butterfly stage.

I was mapping these stages, but I was also walking them. One day I wandered far off campus and came to a construction site which had a quaternity-like foundation with incipient structures. I went to each corner and envisioned the energy of that dimension. Later, I even took a fellow student on this journey who was remarkably open to the experience.

The Australian Aborigine goes on walkabouts to take a break from routine. Paradoxically, the real mandalic walking may begin by a seemingly aimless leaving behind of things. For only in leaving things behind which immerse us, may something new be allowed to emerge. This second doing of "walking" invites to ask where are we on the map of things and to ask where we need to journey next. Sometimes, the seemingly aimless walkabout takes us to a fiery center in which we whirl toward the zone we need to enter.

To give an example, as a high school youth, I was too immersed in the thought world, having excelled academically and in debate, where my partner and I won the state debate championship. In the breakdown experience that followed, I experienced my internal organs melting and that only my clothes were holding me together. After many such experiences, I asked my brother how I had changed after this experience. He told me I showed more emotion in my face. Thus, having gone to one extreme on the mandala of life, I went through a fiery center, which helped transform me into a person more connected with his emotions.

Now, on the mandalic mapping of my time and space, I am in the latter section trying to finish and culminate things, to share what vision I have and what still comes to me. As you age, limitations appear, but they are matched by a relaxed synthetic vision which comes to you more readily after a lifetime of living and work.

So, the second doing presents. Find the map of your life and walk it!

Chapter III

Experiential/Creative Marking

Although we are one of a few billion people, we have unique experiences which make for unique expressions. That newness could arise with each person is a miracle of the infinite wellspring of variety found in the universe. The impulse to be yourself and to express the experiences of the self is envisioned as an essential part of this doing. The specific impulse to make designs, to express our voice in musical sound, or to dance with our unique rhythm is part of this creative, experiential marking. This expression is found in tension and harmony with the cultural norms.

The Indigenous of the world marked stones and rock formations with designs, making for a layer of iconosphere across the surface of the earth. These images included geometric symbolic designs, animals, and anthropomorphs in varying degrees of abstraction. The places inscribed were often by water and in difficult-of-access sites like cliff sides or deep caves. They call to mind our two earlier doings: questing to go to those locations, and their mandalic placement.

The designs drawn were expressive, embodying the naturalistic feel of things, one's own experience of things, and the cultural norms of your group's iconography. Perhaps the most creative/experiential markings are found with anthropomorphs, in which different emotional/spiritual states were conveyed, often with a degree of geometrization. The apparel might present elaborate designs and the body itself overlain with geometric designs. We can surmise that some markings conveyed feelings and experiences that occurred during questing. Interestingly, the word experience has its roots in being "out of peril." Deeply engraved within us are the times when the self is threatened and struggles to overcome obstacles.

Why creatively mark the body, at variance with the norm of appearances? If someone goes through a powerful experience involving direct contact with the spiritual world, there follows a strong urge to assimilate the experience by "creative marking." The person feels a strong impulse to draw, sing, or dance the experience in order to assimilate the impact of such strong realities. "Creative marking," at its heart, is born out of powerful inner transformative experiences.

In my own life, I felt impelled to write about my symbolic experience. After writing it initially, I threw it out as a type of cleansing. But then, regretting that, I began a yearly ritual of rewriting the story, attempting to recreate its order. It was a type of descent into the painfulness and wonder of the experience, which had a price. I wonder as to the purpose now, if it served as an inoculation against further uncontrolled descent. Or perhaps it served to keep sharp the edge used to pierce the veil of the symbolic world.

Once the markings are done, the person's record of the experience can then be reflected upon. It could take a lifetime to discover the meaning of all your experiences, a Jungian analyst once told me. Once the knowledge is gained, the record of the experience can then be shared with others, which may help them in their journey.

One record may have been found on stone I found by the Lower Shenandoah River. Proposed Indigenous markings of a central anthropomorphic form complement the natural beauty of this river cobblestone. The markings speak of a bird-human transformation, a companion spirit, the powerful Ukteni creature, a sinuous form with a bear-like face, and the flower world above. Importantly, the skeletal-like aspect of the anthropomorph, along with its geometricized torso, creates an air of mystery which suggests a transformation event.

In sum, we are called upon and impelled to render our powerful experiences in an expressive way. For example, I have had dreams at night of an inner glowing substance within me that takes on an abstract geometric form. I can write and talk about this dream. We can also be imaged, sung, or danced. When this marking happens, a circle is completed. It is a way of giving thanks for the gift and a prayer that such gifts continue.

Mothering/Mentoring the World

We are called to mother and mentor the world. In a sense we offer our body to the world, just as the mother offers milk for her young. We feed from the world and we are to feed the world back. Perhaps this seems a tall order, a dramatic order, yet it captures an essence of the universe. The alternative is to tear down, to diminish, to belittle others in the world, which ultimately diminishes ourselves more than the object we seek to diminish. We must think of things as being circular, of boomeranging energies, such that what is given is what is returned.

In our awarenesses we have seen how fertility and the importance of female mothering are a high principle for the Indigenous. Now we are called to do what the mother does, to care show love to the young, land, family, and social group.

How does one give of their body, something that is intimate and close to our essence? This giving away can feel like draining and leave one empty, like a husk. Our being will be replenished so we can give again, but significant giving often involves sacrifice. It is something we don't want to do, but it brings life to others. When we have done this giving, we become open and feel a type of ecstasy that fills the emptiness we feel right after giving.

Let us return to the question: How does one give their body? This recalls a dream I had a few years ago of pieces of myself being served in a soup. It sounds cannibalistic, but the feeling of the dream places the meaning on a spiritual plane. How is this done? We do not want to do this; it is something we typically avoid. It seems we have to go against our will in order to give in this way. So, how do we do it? The answer must be that we receive strength from the outside. It is unexpectedly an argument that at the essence of the universe, there is a giving love. Being connected with this, consciously or unconsciously, enables us to give a self-sacrificial love. Thus, Jesus could not have offered himself if he was not connected to the giving essence of the universe. In Christian theological terms, he is one with the giving father/mother, a connection embodied in what is termed the Holy Spirit.

That we can only truly give when we are gifted by outside presence is another great mystery we have come upon. We can mother the world and others in our life if we are connected with and receiving from this giving essence. This gifting being(s) fills and replenishes us after acts of sacrificial love. It raises us from the dead.

When the corn mother is drug around the field seven times, her body is reduced to a skeleton. But she brings life to the fields and her people. Without the mother and her principle, we would not have food to eat, a community, nor life itself. If the Father created the world, the Mother sustains it. We neglect her wisdom at our peril. The irony is that the fathers of the world are called to be mothers, for with the innermost essence of being, there is no separation of the two.

Chapter V

Shamanic Healing

We are called to be healers to ourselves and to one another. In the Indigenous world, the shaman was a designated healer. He or she would travel to other worlds to obtain healing power and energy. The shaman would have an experience in that world, then return with an image, a song, or a word, in order to impart healing to another. That one must go far away to heal someone near at hand is a paradox of the shamanic modality. In a similar way, we can view prayer as trying to access a source that is a step removed from our ordinary consciousness.

We shy away from believing we have healing energy. We wonder, who are we to bring healing to another? Are we that special? Healing comes about because we are a conduit for energy found in another dimension. The question of healing becomes, are we able to be such a conduit? Do we have enough faith and enough centering in our being to tune to these energies?

It's best to remove or minimize ego in any healing attempt/accomplishment. It is best for silence to surround any such miracle, lest healers think they are the source of healing.

Why the impulse to heal? First, persons ask for healing. It is a demand made from a personal entity in the universe. Sometimes, the demand is unspoken, a silent scream. We hear it if we listen with our soul. Perhaps the best healers are the ones who address the unspoken demand. Thus, demands present, and the question becomes how do we respond?

A good healer listens, picks up cries in silence, and addresses them. When we see or meet a person, perhaps that should be a question we ask ourselves. In what way does this person need healing? There are many thoughts that can run through one's mind, but why should this not be one of them? If persons I meet have this thought and intention, would I not be drawn to them?

The healing response may simply be a kind word, a note of encouragement, or pointing gently to a new direction. We must awaken this healer within us and act with healing intentions if our world is going to survive. The alternative is to move in the other direction, of habitually putting down people or groups of people, of making them an object of sarcasm and belittlement. Why choose the way of laughter at others, rather than embracing a pain that can be turned to joy? What words will be left or said about us after we die? Will they be, "He was really tough and mean to those who got in his way?" Or will they be, "He tried to love all, even those who hurt him?"

Healing is an act of love that enters into another's pain. This empathic response comes at a cost which the healer endures for love of the other. When the person in need of healing realizes another loves him or her enough to enter their pain, half the healing is done. The other half comes from the Source of Life itself, upon which disease, death, and pain have no hold.

All this is about faith, one might object. You imagine a Source of Healing; you imagine persons believing they can impart such energy. You believe that people have empathic bones in their bodies. This is all true, that "shamanic healing" relies heavily relies on belief. But this reliance does not mean that it is not true and that it will not work.

If belief is at the essence of much of this, we might ask: where does that come from? Can I believe that I can be a force for the healing of others? Belief itself is said to be a gift, for our practical minds hem in the realm of possibility and imagination. For now, all I can say is to try the healing way. Believe you can do good, that you can access power greater than yourself and that good can result. When you meet a person, ask what healing they need and how you might be a part of that. If need be, spend a quiet moment, and ask for help in the matter.

Chapter VI

Seek Being

Our last doing embraces a paradox. We are called to seek Being. Seeking means searching, longing, wondering about, and attempting to embrace. All the doings are wrapped together in this: vision questing, mandalic walking, creative marking, mentoring the world, and shamanic healing. All of these efforts are meant to draw ourselves and others closer to Being.

"What is Being?" we are led to ask. We sense that it is something full, has presence, and is loving. We can feel and discern this Source as personal, and as the height of abstraction, as having human form and being beyond form. Perhaps the greatest mystery of Being is its hiddenness, its humility. Though Being can be viewed as the Source of all things and the end to which all things go, it does not impose itself. How can this be? Does Being, at its essence, like loving surprise?

But does Being exist? All the great religions believe in some way of the existence of deep Being. The Indigenous too often hold a belief in a great overarching Spirit, such *Wakan Tanka* with the Lakota. Nonetheless, the existence of Being remains unproven in standard overt ways of proving. Being is something experienced, like love. We cannot prove that love exists, but we can feel it. We cannot show it directly, but we act under its influence. It is respect for the independence of our being that Being does not show itself directly. Mystical experiences approach this, although they are, in all likelihood, but fringes of the divine Being.

We are meant to approach Being, but we cannot fully immerse into it until we die. Our being in its current form cannot absorb the full reality of Being. In order to fully experience Being, our current body must be shed, and a new body/being emerge.

All this you may object is faith dependent, speculative, and has its origins in a particular religious slant. My answer is that it arises from a lifetime, which is hurling toward its conclusion. It is informed by all my explorations including detailed study of biology/evolution, the deep psyche of the human, the wisdom of the Indigenous, the experience of the world's beauty as revealed by photography, the imaginative realm of fiction, and my own life experience. This is what I have come to believe and hope for.

I once had a conversation with my brother John, in which I revealed that I believe in life after death, but I am not absolutely sure. It is a faith. My brother, who held such certitude, answered, "If it's not true, it should be so." At any rate, I believe we live a fuller life with the realization and thankfulness that we come from Being and that we go to Being after our death.

It is a paradox that something so near can seem so far away. We draw a breath and our existence continues, in all but a miracle. We must be connected to Being in the most intimate way, even in order for our physical being to exist, yet we must extend ourselves to become aware of Being.

We are called to seek Being, and in doing so we approach the ultimate mystery of our existence and that of the universe. We approach the Way we should live, the Way to give life as Being does. First seek Being and all else will be given to you!

CONCLUSION

We are called to be aware and called to do. The two are integrated, for as we become aware, we are led to do. Then our doing delves us deeper into awareness of our world. Awareness congruent with doing leads us to a full life. We are led into Being, in which our sense of Presence increases from our awareness-doing. We will increasingly feel ecstatic states mixing with the ordinary of our day.

Ultimately, life is about connection, joining, and love. There is no separation from Love or Being, and we culminate and hurl toward those ends. This is a grand conclusion, but it is our conclusion to which we should aspire.

Perhaps it would be a good exercise to offer ourselves up every day to Being and Love. For what other purpose would we live? Would we live to diminish and hate? Could we hope to win by taking the dark path, when so much Being and Love are around us? For every breath we take, every portion of food we eat, every good word or deed we receive from another are keeping us alive this day. We cannot predict where this good will come from, either. Except we know that lowly plants, creatures, and persons have their portion of good to give. The gifts can even come from the Indigenous, as we've seen in this work. And finally on this list, we should not forget the Presence of humble Being and Love, the Source and End of All.

It is hard to write the final thought, for the good is infinite and Love has no end. We will each add to the story. Our awarenesses and doings will always keep growing, and the circle of love will keep expanding. Death will not stop it. For our part, let us continue to accept the gifts tossed extravagantly our way.

Don't miss out!

Visit the website below and you can sign up to receive emails whenever Michael A. Susko publishes a new book. There's no charge and no obligation.

https://books2read.com/r/B-A-GJLJ-AYSAC

BOOKS2READ

Connecting independent readers to independent writers.

Did you love *Gifts from the Indigenous: Another Way of Viewing &* *Acting in the World*? Then you should read *Mystery Stone from the Shenandoah: Analyzed with Eastern Woodland Cosmology*[1] by Michael A. Susko!

[2]

A beautiful tablet-like mystery stone has been found by the Shenandoah River, near Berryville, Virginia. Underneath its brown-orange patina, peck-marked shapes reveal a crystalline heartstone underneath and intriguing designs. Varied opinions have been offered by experts on the oriign of the designs, so the author takes you on a tour of the stone so you can make your own judgement. He illustrates surprising gestalts, their aesthetic nature, and how they resonate with Eastern Woodland cosmology of early America. They include the presence of a pervasive spiritual energy, the tension and complementariness of twins, and forms

---

1. https://books2read.com/u/b5XopA

2. https://books2read.com/u/b5XopA

which suggest the archetypes of avian-man, earth mother, and skeletal shaman. With profuse images supported by commentary, we explore an alternative way to view the universe, and one that can enrich our lives.

Read more at https://www.allroneofus.com/.

Also by Michael A. Susko

A Couple Through Time
Down Below & the Archon's Castle
Up Above & the Runaway
Across the Gulf & Journey Into Un-Time
On the Bay & a Child Found
Down New River & Another World
In the Wild & Do One Wild Thing
On the Mountain & Two Are Missing
To the Beginning & Journey Through Here

Archetypal Worlds
Giant Under the Mountain & the Mystery of Sacrifice
The Alien's Gift
The Gold People
Spider Woman and the Timeroc
Darkwood and Dual with the Shadow Side
Quill Ears & the Other Earth
Alwon in Another World: An Archetypal Voyage
Line In the Wall

Beyond and a New World

Beyond & a New World: I Cosmos
Beyond & A New World: II Bios
Beyond & a New World: III Mythos
Beyond & A New World: IV Logos

Biographic Book of Tens

Ten Discoveries from Biology to Spirituality: Hidden & Life-Giving Connections
Ten Times We Almost Died
Ten Sayings to Guide Our Lives
Ten Mystery Photos: Personal & Cosmological Reflections
Ten Mementos on Our Desk: Remembering Moments
Ten Metadiscoveries We Have Made

Four Years

A Survival Manual for the Next Four Years
What—Me Worry? The Next Four Years
Flirting with the Fox: The Next Four Years
New Holidays are Coming! The Next Four Years
New Monuments are Coming! The Next Four Years
New Bible Stories are Coming! The Next Four Years
New Fairy Tales Are Coming! The Next Four Years
Why I Don't Need to Repent: Four More Years!

Haikus and Photos

Flowers and Haikus
Haikus and Photos: Guatemalan Highlands
Haikus and Photos: Water Birds and Reflections
Haikus and Photos: Seasons of New River
Haikus and Photos: Yosemite Wilderness
Haikus and Photos: California Coast
Haikus and Photos: Canadian Rockies
Haikus and Photos: Hawaii's Exotic Landscapes
Haikus and Photos: Vienna: People, Buildings and Art
Haikus and Photos: Slovakian Castles and Hamlets
Haikus and Photos: Berlin, Light and Dark
Haikus and Photos: New Orleans, City of Immigrants
Haikus and Photos: Antietam Wind and Spirits
Haikus & Photos: Plant Abstractions
Haikus and Photos: Appalachian Beauty
Haikus and Photos: Urban Farm in Sandtown
Haikus and Photos: New York Heights and Ground
Haikus & Photos: Santa Fe Fractal-Pueblo Spirtuality
Haikus and Photos: Monticello's Double Vision

Little Lion
The Lion and the Chameleon
The Elephant and the Chameleons
Little Lion and His Friends
Little Lion In Flower World
Gurr in Arid Land
Little Dragon Goes to China

Logarithmic Evolutionary Time

On the Mountain & To the Beginning

Rosetta Key
A Rosetta Key for History: Generations Revealing the Phases of Time
A Rosetta Key For U.S. History: Renewal or Rigidification?
A Rosetta Key for Ancestral Pueblo History: Phases of an Indigenous
Civilization

Second Mystery Stone from the Shenandoah
Haikus & Photos: 2nd Shenandoan Mystery Stone
Haikus and Photos: 2nd Mystery Stone 3-D Forms

Servants of the Flower World
Flower Amid the Devastation: Servants of the Flower World, Book I
Questers in Flower World: Servants of the Flower World, Book II
Fight for This World: Servants of the Flower World, Book III
Journey to the Underworld & The Circle of Emptiness
The Edge of Return

Shenandoan Stone Explorations
Mystery Stone from the Shenandoah: Analyzed with Eastern
Woodland Cosmology
Philosopher Stone from the Lower Shenandoah
Beyond the Portal: From Within the Mystery Stone
The Mystery of Essence

Gifts from the Indigenous: Another Way of Viewing & Acting in the World

Shenandoan Stone: Haikus & Photos
Haikus and Photos: Cosmogram from the Shenandoah
Haikus and Photos: Woodland Mystery Stone and World Archetypes
Haikus and Photos: Skeletal Human and Mississippian Art
Haikus and Photos: Mystery Stone's Animal Forms
Haikus and Photos: Plant Forms and Mystery Stone

Stone Formation at Penn Bluff
Haikus and Photos: Presence at Penn Bluff
Haikus & Photos: Mystery Forms at Penn Bluff
Haikus and Photos: Essences at Penn Bluff
Haikus and Photos: World Archetypes at Penn Bluff

The Dreaming Series
Sleek Back & Salamander Dreaming
Streak & Cave Bear Dreaming
Moby & Marsupial Mole Dreaming

The Dream World Trilogy
Delphi, the Time Thief, and the Dream World
Detinna and the Cave God
The Resistance & the Empire

Transformational Stories
Caseness and Narrative: Contrasting Approaches to People
Psychiatrically Labeled
Transformative Experiences, Psychiatric Research, and Informed
Consent
Transformational Stories: Voices for True Healing in Mental Health

Worlds to the Side
A Couple Through Time, I. From Down Below to On the Bay
A Couple Through Time, II From Down New River to Journey
Through Here

Writings from Street People
Street Images
Street Images II

Standalone
Little People & the Curious Time-Riding Animal
Animal Spell: A Journey Through Darkness & Light
Child of the Elements
The Firekeeper & The Spirit of the Long Night
Life's Dynamic Vulnerability, and Its Natural Extravagance
Alien Ally
The Generation of Life: Imagery, Ritual and Experiences in Deep Caves
Twelve Suspects: And the Case of the Missing Body
2084: Clash of Cults

Bats in the Future
Guard of the Dead & Servant of the Living
The Imagination Being
Ten Traits of Empire That Every Person Should Know
Aging and Renewal: Actualizing Our LIves
The Meaning, Beauty & Mystery of Dreams: Seven Guidelines and
Seven Tools for Listening
The Fragility of Evolution: Re-envisioning Life's Creative Processes
Ways We May Be Surprised by Heaven
Why Go Slow When You Can Hurl to Your Destruction?
Stages of the Human Life Cycle: A Novel Logarithmic Perspective
Fifteen Amazing Things About the Body
The Human Body as Evolutionary Treasures
What does ChatGPT see in the Mystery Photos?
Agents of Immortality: Six Ways To Living Forever
The Logarithmic Nature of Time: From the Start of Life to Symbolizing
Humanity
Animal Dreaming: The Adventures of Finn
Chameleon Adventures
Dream World Trilogy
As Lover, Lion, & Phoenix
Generational Key to History: Tracing Phases From Ancient Egypt to
America
Planetary Revolution: The Next Stage in Human Awareness!
Down Below to the Beginning
New Ways Are Coming! The Next Four Years
Seven Ways to Prove You're a Christian Leader
From Sunfish to Son: The Gifts of Our Lives
Cosmos & Bios: Beyond & a New World
Astronomical & Biological Unfolding of Time
Servants of the Flower World: Book I-III
Mystery Photos: Human & AI Reflections
Down Below to a New World: A Couple Through Time

Watch for more at https://www.allroneofus.com/.

About the Author

After having gone through a symbolic, quest experience, the author obtained degrees in Philosophy and Counseling Psychology. For many years, he taught a course on Indigenous symbolism. Having encounters with the sacred in the landscapes of the Shenandoah Valley, northern Alabama, and Guatemala, he offers this work as *Gifts from the Indigenous.*

Read more at https://www.allroneofus.com/.

About the Publisher

AllRoneof Us Publishing seeks out work that offers a novel and qualitative contribution to world literature—the kind of work that may endure across generations.

We are especially drawn to voices that are often underheard, overlooked, or nearly lost—including authors in the later chapters of life who have made exemplary contributions that remain unrecognized. Our imprint serves as a sanctuary for works of insight, humanity, and lasting value.

Among those we have been honored to publish, we recommend:*Rich Mullin's Ethics and the Full-Breasted Richness of Life*,*John Susko's Flowers of the Night: Musings from a Sentimental Son*,and *Dr. Curtis Adams' Psychosis and the Humpty Dumpty Story*.

www.ingramcontent.com/pod-product-compliance
Lightning Source LLC
Chambersburg PA
CBHW021320160726
47994CB00004B/1532